21st
Century
Skills Library

POWER UP!

COAL

ROBERT GREEN

Published in the United States of America by
Cherry Lake Publishing, Ann Arbor, Michigan
www.cherrylakepublishing.com

Content Adviser
Allison Hein, Research Engineer, Institute of Materials Processing,
Michigan Technological University

Credits
Photos: Cover and page 1, ©James M. Phelps, Jr, used under license from
Shutterstock, Inc.; page 4, ©iStockphoto.com/acilo; page 7, ©jeremy sutton-hibbert/
Alamy; page 8, ©bierchen, used under license from Shutterstock, Inc.; page 10,
©iStockphoto.com/MikLav; page 12, Roberto Castillo, used under license from
Shutterstock, Inc.; page 13, ©H. Mark Weidman Photography/Alamy; page 14,
©Lianem/Dreamstime.com; pages 16 and 24, ©Mike Goldwater/Alamy; page 18,
©A.S. Zain, used under license from Shutterstock, Inc.; page 21, ©iStockphoto.com/
bncc369; page 22, Semen Lixodeev, used under license from Shutterstock, Inc.;
page 23, © Phil Degginger/Alamy; page 27, ©Brian A Jackson, used under
license from Shutterstock, Inc.; page 28, ©airphoto.gr, used under license from
Shutterstock, Inc.; page 29, ©Jim West/Alamy

Library of Congress Cataloging-in-Publication Data
Green, Robert, 1969–
  Coal / by Robert Green.
      p. cm.—(Power up!)
  Includes index.
  ISBN-13: 978-1-60279-508-2
  ISBN-10: 1-60279-508-8
  1. Coal—Juvenile literature. I. Title.
II. Series.
  TN801.G74 2009
  553.2'4—dc22   2008044184

Cherry Lake Publishing would like to acknowledge
the work of The Partnership for 21st Century Skills.
Please visit *www.21stcenturyskills.org* for more information.

POWER UP!

TABLE OF CONTENTS

CHAPTER ONE
AN UNUSUAL ENERGY SOURCE

With the flip of a light switch, a house becomes a magic place. Electricity charges into lightbulbs, and night becomes as bright as day. Electricity keeps milk

Power lines bring electricity to houses, offices, schools, and other buildings.

from spoiling in the refrigerator. It runs fans and air conditioners that keep your house cool in the summer months. It also runs the computers you use every day. So where does all that electricity come from? The answer might surprise you.

If you walk around outside your house or apartment building, you will discover wires running into the building. Some of these are for cable TV, and some are for the telephone. But there will always be at least one wire for the electricity, which runs everything in the house.

These wires carry electricity from a vast network of connected wires called a power grid. Electricity travels along these wires to power an entire area. If you were to follow the electricity backward from your house, you would end up at a power plant where electricity is produced.

Power can be made in different ways. The most common way to produce electricity is to burn coal.

A simple fire at the heart of a power station is needed to make electricity. That fire burns the black rocklike substance known as coal. Coal doesn't look very special. It doesn't shine like a diamond or have the bright color of an emerald. It is usually black in color, though sometimes brownish, and messy to touch. It looks like charcoal but is generally harder.

Before the coal is burned, it is crushed into tiny bits almost like dust. This crushed coal is then loaded into furnaces, where it is burned to produce electricity.

Coal is found all over the world. China digs up the most coal from the earth every year, followed by the United States, Australia, and India. If you were to fly in a plane at night and circle the globe, you would see lights burning in cities all around the world. Most of those lights are the result of coal-burning electrical plants.

21ST CENTURY CONTENT

One negative result of burning coal is pollution. Burning coal creates gases such as carbon dioxide that are harmful to the environment. What happens when we don't want the pollution, but need the coal for jobs and electricity?

China is the biggest producer of carbon dioxide pollution today. The second-biggest producer is the United States. U.S. leaders want China to stop polluting so much. But China has 1 billion more people than the United States. Per person, Americans cause much more pollution than the Chinese. Is it fair for less populated countries to criticize more populated countries about pollution? Why or why not?

Coal miners wait at the entrance to a mine shaft. Their work shift will soon begin.

CHAPTER TWO
JUST HOW OLD IS THAT COAL?

We have seen that coal can do some surprising things despite its common appearance. The black, dusty rock helps turn on lights around the world. So just where does this important rock come from?

Peat is close to the surface and relatively easy to dig up. It is left to dry in rows or piles before being sold as fuel or for other uses.

Its story is just as surprising. Coal is a lifeless rock that comes from plants that lived millions of years ago. To understand how that is possible, it is important to remember that Earth changes over time. Areas where coal is found might be wooded, or they might be dry, hilly landscapes. No matter where coal is found, you can count on one thing: millions of years ago, there was a swamp on that spot. Without swamps, there would be no coal.

Swamps create a set of conditions necessary to produce coal. When plants in swamps die, some of the plant matter sinks into the earth at the bottom of the swamp. The plant matter is slowly covered by layers of matter from other dying plants. Over time, this forms a dense layer of dead plant remains known as peat. Peat was used as an energy source by ancient people. They dug it out of the peat bogs and swamps, and burned it to create heat.

Over millions of years, the layers of peat continued to sink beneath other layers of new peat or dirt. As more layers built up, the bottom layers of dead plant matter were subjected to heat and pressure. The heat and pressure caused the layers to harden into a more rocklike substance, which we know as coal.

There are different types of coal. The differences arise from the age of the coal, how much **carbon** it contains, and how the heat and pressure have affected it. As a layer of coal continues to sink, the earth above it presses down with even greater weight. As a result, newer coal is not as hard as older coal underneath it.

The youngest coal is produced from plants that lived about 1 million years ago. It is called **lignite**. Lignite is crumbly and moist, brownish in color, and usually found close to the earth's surface. It is commonly burned in power plants to create electricity.

This lignite mine is in Germany. Lignite is lighter in color and softer than black coal.

Coal from older layers beneath the ground is known as **subbituminous coal**. Still older layers than that give us **bituminous coal**. Bituminous coal is the most plentiful kind of coal in the United States. It was formed by plants that lived about 300 million years ago.

There is one even older and harder form of coal, known as **anthracite**. What makes anthracite the hardest kind of coal? It is the amount of pressure over time that pressed the once-living plant matter into a very hard black rock.

Anthracite is made mainly of carbon. This **element** contains stored energy from the days when the plants soaked up the rays of the sun. It was the carbon in the peat that allowed ancient people to use it for fires. And as the peat sunk beneath the ground, it was pressed into purer and purer forms of carbon.

Piles of coal are ready for shipment outside a coal mine.

Mines in Pennsylvania, such as this one, produce most of the world's anthracite.

Nearer the surface, lignite contains about 25 to 35 percent carbon. Hard and very ancient anthracite can be 86 to 97 percent carbon. It is that concentration of carbon, formed over millions of years, that makes coal a good source of energy.

CHAPTER THREE
GOING TO GROUND

Without ancient swamps, we would have no coal to use for electricity. But the formation of coal presents a problem because coal lies under the ground we walk on.

To get to the coal, human beings become like burrowing animals. Perhaps you've seen a burrowing animal—a chipmunk,

A surface mine can look like it is surrounded by steps. These were created as miners dug through layers of earth.

a badger, or a groundhog—in action. These animals dig holes or tunnels into the earth.

Humans use all kinds of machines and different kinds of technology to help dig the coal out of the ground. Coal miners are the people who dig for coal. The type of machines they use depends on the type of coal being dug up.

Coal can be found at different levels beneath the ground. Harder coal is deeper underground. Soft, crumbly coal is closer to the surface. The good news for coal miners is that the coal was formed in layers. Once coal is discovered, there is usually a wide area to mine. This is known as a coal seam, which is just another way of saying a layer of coal under the ground.

Coal miners use two techniques to dig up the coal, depending on how deep underground it is. The first type of mining is surface mining, in which miners dig up shallower beds of coal. These coal beds are not actually on the surface but are buried under layers of earth. The miners must strip away these layers of dirt to reveal the bed of coal beneath. The miners then dig up the coal using giant machines. After the coal is removed, the miners fill in the hole with the original soil to restore the land. Generally, trees are then planted to keep the soil from washing away.

Surface mining can be done on coal beds within 200 feet (61 meters) of Earth's surface. To reach coal deeper than 200 feet, miners use the second technique: underground mining, or deep mining. The miners make tunnels just like burrowing animals. The tunnels are called mine shafts. Shafts can run in different directions. The miners first determine where the coal seam is and then decide how to reach it.

For example, if coal is discovered in a mountain, miners can dig sideways into the mountain and dig out the coal from the side. If the coal seam is deep underground, the miners will dig a deep mine shaft straight down into the ground. Miners then build an elevator in the mine shaft. They ride that

Miners who work underground wear hard hats and safety glasses. Their hats have lights attached to help them see.

elevator down to the coal deposit. When they arrive, they dig out the coal and send it back up the elevator.

Traveling deep into the ground to mine coal is much more dangerous than surface mining. Miners have to be very careful that they don't cause the ground to fall in as they dig out the coal. Miners must work carefully and always follow safety rules.

Unlike surface mining, underground mining only disturbs a small area of land on the surface. The mine might have only a few small entrances aboveground but stretch for miles below the earth.

LIFE & CAREER SKILLS

Mining is a dangerous job. Some mining accidents are caused by a collapse in the tunnel. Dangerous gases such as methane and carbon monoxide can cause explosions or prevent miners from getting enough oxygen to survive. A long time ago, one simple safety measure was to bring canaries into the mine. Canaries are sensitive to methane and carbon monoxide. If the birds stopped singing, the miners knew they had to get out of the mine. Today, miners use sensors to make sure the air in mines is safe. They use roof supports to keep the ceiling from collapsing.

CHAPTER FOUR
FROM COAL TO ENERGY

Once the coal is separated from dirt at the mine, it is transported to a power plant. This can be done by train or by boat if there is a river nearby. At the power plant,

Coal can be transported by river on barges.
Tugboats are often used to push them along.

the coal is crushed into tiny pieces. This process is known as **pulverization**. It turns the coal into something like dust, which can be burned more easily than large pieces of coal.

We know that coal is burned in a very hot fire to produce electricity. Can you imagine just how this might work? Coal is burned to release heat, but electricity doesn't come from heat. The heat is used to boil water and produce steam in the furnace of a power plant. Water pipes pass near the heat of the furnace. When the water in the pipes gets hot enough, steam is created.

The steam is then pumped into a **turbine**, or spinning machine. The steam causes the machine to turn around and around. So steam from the heat of the furnace runs a machine that produces **mechanical energy**. It is the mechanical energy from the spinning of the machine that generates electricity.

The electricity that comes from the turbine runs through wires that come out of the power plant. These wires carry the electricity along a network of wires to the users of electricity. This network of wires is often referred to as the power grid. There are users of electricity in almost every house and building.

About half of the electricity used in the United States comes from coal-burning power plants. In some countries, coal is even more important. China uses more coal every year than any other country. It relies on coal for almost 70 percent of its electricity.

Electricity is so important that most of the coal we dig up is sent to power plants. For example, more than 90 percent of all the coal dug up in the United States is burned at electric power plants. But coal has other uses as well. The 10 percent that is not burned for electricity is still very important to modern life.

LEARNING & INNOVATION SKILLS

The heat released from burning coal is a kind of energy called **thermal energy**. Unfortunately, most of that energy is lost, and the heat escapes into the surrounding environment. Many experts work to solve this problem of wasted energy. Today, new technologies have been developed that allow companies to make use of that wasted energy. For example, heat released from burning coal can be moved around a building through a heating system. That heat can keep the building warm during the winter. The extra heat can also be used to heat the water used by the people who work in the building.

Some of the thermal energy produced when coal is burned escapes into the environment.

What are some of the other ways people use coal? One example is concrete, which is used to make buildings and sidewalks. Concrete is made in factories that need a lot of heat. That heat comes from furnaces that are fueled by coal. Paper is another common product that requires a lot of heat to make. That heat also comes from coal burned in furnaces.

Coal is needed to make steel, which is used to make cars and many other products. To make steel, coal is first burned

Factories use coal to produce the heat needed to make paper.

Very high temperatures are needed to melt the iron that is used to make steel.

at high temperatures to form a substance known as **coke**. This is a hardened mixture of coal and ash. The coke is used to heat the fires that turn iron ore into iron. Iron is then used to make steel.

As you can see, coal is used in different ways. It is clear that coal plays an important role in shaping the world around us.

CHAPTER FIVE
A FUTURE WITH COAL

In the search for energy, coal is plentiful. It can be found under the ground in countries all over the world. Once it is found, there is often a lot of it to dig up in one spot. It is

Masks help keep some coal dust out of miners' lungs, but not all of it.

cheap compared to other forms of energy, and it is easy to turn into electricity.

Yet coal has its problems, too. Coal's biggest problem is that it is a messy source of energy and a major cause of pollution. Coal is messy at almost all stages of its production and use. When miners dig up coal and crush it into tiny pieces, the coal dust gets in their lungs. This can cause breathing problems and other health problems. Miners have to wear masks and use various methods to keep coal dust out of the air.

Coal dust can also seep into rivers and into the soil. This can harm plants and animals. These are all problems that occur before coal is burned in a power plant. The worst pollution caused by coal comes from the burning itself.

When coal is burned, it releases emissions (gases and particles) into the air. These emissions include substances that cause harm to the air and water. For example, **mercury** is released when coal from certain mines is burned. The mercury floats into the air and eventually lands on the earth again. The mercury builds up in rivers and lakes. It can poison fish and other living things in the water. The mercury can also poison people who eat the fish.

Burning coal releases carbon dioxide, a gas that traps heat in the atmosphere. This makes Earth's atmosphere like a greenhouse that traps heat. Gases, such as carbon dioxide, that cause this effect are known as greenhouse gases. Scientists believe that greenhouse gases are causing Earth's atmosphere to warm and are causing global climate change. This is known as global warming. Global warming causes ice to melt in the polar ice caps, resulting in higher water levels in the ocean. Just think about what would happen if you lived near an ocean and it continued to rise. Eventually, your home would be underwater. Global warming can also cause many other problems, such as the growth of deserts and the drying out of farmland.

21ST CENTURY CONTENT

Fossil fuels such as coal and oil are nonrenewable energy resources. This means that they can be used up over time. Both coal and oil form naturally, but the process takes millions of years. Once the supplies are gone, we cannot wait around for them to form again.

Today, scientists are turning to renewable sources of energy. These are energy sources that can't be used up. For example, energy from the sun can be turned into electricity. Wind energy can be harnessed and turned into energy. Developing ways to get energy from renewable resources is helping to reduce pollution and create alternatives to coal and oil.

Wind can be used to turn turbines and generate electricity.

To prevent the negative effects of burning coal, filters are used to clean the smoke as it comes out of a power plant. This technology helps prevent the harmful parts of the smoke from polluting the environment. But it does not stop all of the pollution.

The smoke coming from a power plant may look clean, but it still contains some harmful pollutants.

These students are against building more coal power plants. Now that you know more about coal, what do you think?

Scientists are working on new ways to get power from coal without creating so much pollution. New clean coal technologies include different ways of burning coal and cleaning up after the coal is burned. Coal causes less pollution when it is burned in a liquid form or as a gas. These technologies are expensive, but they might help coal become less harmful to the environment. They could help make coal a better energy alternative for the 21st century.

GLOSSARY

anthracite (AN-thruh-site) one of the hardest forms of coal with a very high carbon content

bituminous coal (bih-TOO-muh-nuss KOHL) a type of coal that has a higher carbon content and burns easily

carbon (KAR-buhn) an extremely common element that forms organic compounds and is the primary element of coal

coke (KOHK) the remains of coal burned at high temperatures

element (EL-uh-muhnt) a substance that cannot be separated into simpler substances

lignite (LIG-nite) a soft brownish black coal

mechanical energy (muh-KAN-uh-kuhl EN-ur-jee) energy that results from the movement of a machine, such as a turbine

mercury (MUR-kyuh-ree) a highly toxic metallic element that can be released into the air when coal is burned

pulverization (puhl-ver-ih-ZAY-shuhn) the crushing of a substance, such as coal, into a fine powder

subbituminous coal (sub-bih-TOO-muh-nuss KOHL) a form of coal harder than lignite but softer than bituminous coal that is often used in coal-fired electrical power plants

thermal energy (THUR-muhl EN-ur-jee) energy that results from heat

turbine (TUR-bine) a machine with a spinning part that can produce electricity and is sometimes powered by steam

FOR MORE INFORMATION

BOOKS

Haugen, David M. (editor). *Coal*. Detroit: Greenhaven Press, 2006.

Johnson, Rebecca L. *Investigating Climate Change: Scientists' Search for Answers in a Warming World*. Minneapolis: Twenty-First Century Books, 2009.

WEB SITES

Energy Kid's Page—Coal
www.eia.doe.gov/kids/energyfacts/sources/non-renewable/coal.html
Read more about how coal is formed and what it is used for

The EPA Climate Change Kids Site
www.epa.gov/climatechange/kids/
Information about global climate change and links to games and other activities

HowStuffWorks—How Power Grids Work
www.howstuffworks.com/power.htm
Watch a video that explains how the U.S. power grid works

INDEX

ABOUT THE AUTHOR

Robert Green has written more than 30 books for students. He is a regular contributor to publications by the Economist Intelligence Unit and holds graduate degrees from New York University and Harvard.